Social Learning Profile

A team discussion tool for the development of respectful and successful behavioral plans for individuals with special needs and those who support them.

Jeff Jacobs, Greg Cardelli, Doug Boeckmann

AAPCPUBLISHING
EMBRACING NEURODIVERSITY

PO BOX 861116
Shawnee, KS 66286
www.aapcautismbooks.com

Publisher's Cataloging-In-Publication

Names: Jacobs, Jeff (Jeffrey Alan), author. | Cardelli, Greg, author. | Boeckmann, Doug, author.

Title: Social learning profile : a team discussion tool for the development of respectful and successful behavioral plans for individuals with special needs and those who support them / Jeff Jacobs, Greg Cardelli, Doub Boeckmann.

Description: Shawnee, KS : AAPC Publishing, [2022]

Identifiers: ISBN: 9781956110135 (paperback)

Subjects: LCSH: Social learning. | Social skills. | Socialization. | Children with disabilities--Behavior modification. | Children with disabilities--Life skills guides. | Children with autism spectrum disorders--Behavior modifiction. | Children with autism spectrum disorders--Life skills guides. | People with disabilities--Behavior modification. | People with disabilities--Life skills guides. | Autistic people--Behavior modification. | Autistic people--Life skills guides. | Teachers of children with disabilities--Handbooks, manuals, etc. | Parents of children with disabilities--Handbooks, manuals, etc.

Classification: LCC: LC192.4 .J33 2022 | DDC: 303.32--dc23

Dedication

We are indebted to the excellent teachers, paraprofessionals, administrators, and support staff that we have had the great privilege to work with and learn from for more than forty years.

We are indebted to the parents of our students, the true experts, whose insights and advocacy keep us all on the right path.

And most of all, we are indebted to our students, who taught us everything we know.

CONTENTS

Section IV / Values Check

Section V / Writing the Social Learning Profile

Section VI / A Simple Data Keeping System

Introduction

When we change the way that we look at things, the things we look at change. - Wayne Dyer

A person's behavior is like a clue in a mystery story. It reveals and it conceals. It leads and it misleads. It speaks a variety of messages and serves a variety of purposes. It is affected by the situations in which it occurs, the response that it receives, and the depth of the need that it conveys. It is as complex as the person who uses it, and who is, too often, defined by it.

This can be especially true for someone with special needs, who might not always be able to tell us what's *wrong*, what they *need*, or how to *help.*

Sometimes, a person's behavior can be so confusing (and so frustrating) that it is tempting to reach for easy answers and quick solutions. As the mother of one of our students once put it, perhaps only half-seriously, *"I wish that my son had come with instructions!"* We do not presume to provide those instructions, but, instead, to provide a clear and respectful process by which that mother, and her son's team, can find their *own* answers and write their *own* instructions.

The process that you have before you is a team discussion tool for the development of respectful and successful behavioral plans for persons with special needs (and those who support them). It is user-friendly, non-technical, jargon-free, and respectful of the individual dignity and feelings of everyone involved. The source of its information and knowledge is the person's own team, and its purpose is to facilitate that team's discussion.

A Team Discussion Tool.

There is no "I" in the team.

This process is designed as a series of team discussion questions. It asks rather than tells, and it seeks to find its answers within the collective observations, insights, and experiences of the people who know the student best - his or her team. It is intended to get people talking to each other, not to tell them what to do.

It has been our experience that the answers to even the most complex and challenging of behavioral issues can usually be found within the combined wisdom of the team, and that if asked the *right questions*, they can usually find the *right answers* on their own.

The *questions themselves* are respectful and easy to answer. They are intended to be as comfortable being discussed around a kitchen table as around a conference table. Even the order of the questions is designed to make the process more comfortable.

Most schools and organizations have their own rules for determining who is a part of the team. That usually includes the student themselves, their parents or guardians, and the professionals who support them. Just be sure to include the people who know the student best, even if they disagree with each other (and perhaps, especially if they disagree with each other).

So, as it turns out, there actually is an "I" in team. In fact, there are many of them, each with their own perspectives and feelings that must be listened to and respected if the team is to accomplish its purpose.

Respectful, Non-Technical Language

To produce a dignified result, use a dignified process - Dr. John McGee.

The words that we use when talking about a person's behavior, when addressing a person who is having a behavioral difficulty, or when explaining his or her behavior to others, can all have a profound impact upon the person him or herself, on those watching from the sidelines, and ultimately on our own actions.

Consider for example, how differently you might respond if asked to help a student who was *having* a problem, as opposed to a student who was *causing* a problem. And that is a difference of only *one word*!

The words used throughout this process are designed to spring from a sense of respect for the individual dignity of the person who is being discussed, empathy for their personal struggle, and an understanding of the underlying needs which are being manifested through their behavior. When discussing a student's behavior, we will only use words that we would not mind hearing spoken about our own sons, daughters, nieces, or nephews.

Finally, throughout the process, we use the term "individual"," "student," or "person" interchangeably to indicate the person who is at the heart of our discussion, but we could just as easily say son, daughter, client, patient, or any of the other titles that we accumulate in life. We encourage you, the reader, to substitute the *first name* of the person that *you* have in mind.

The Process Itself

Seek first to understand - Steven Covey

This process is designed to be clear and simple in its framework. It is divided into six sections:

Section I. **Areas of Need or Difficulty** (The Stress & Behavior Profile): An assessment tool that examines specific behaviors, problems, or stressors, and the context in which they occur.

Section II. **Success Strategies**: A collection of preventive and educative strategies that are designed to increase the likelihood of a student's success, and thereby make behaviors, problems, and stressors less likely to occur.

Section III. **Calming & Coping Strategies**: A set of practical calming techniques that help a student to relax and regroup during times of stress and distress.

Section IV. **Values Check**: A self-evaluation tool for ensuring that our strategies and plans are in keeping with our own values, professional best practices, and community standards.

Section V. **Writing the Social Learning Profile**: A short section that offers guidance and structure on producing a written document that can be shared with others.

Section VI. **A Simple Data Keeping Tool**: A simple and effective tool for measuring success and evaluating outcomes.

Each section begins with a *one-page* set of team discussion questions, followed by a corresponding set of supplementary checklists or examples. The entire process is *fully contained* within the team discussion questions on just four pages (16, 35, 59, and 81). Everything else (the checklists, explanation sheets, data collection tools, etc.) are all just there to support those questions.

Section I

Areas of Need or Difficulty

(The Stress and Behavior Profile)

Section I

Areas of Need or Difficulty

(The Stress & Behavior Profile)

For every complex problem, there is a solution that is simple, easy, and wrong - H.L. Mencken

Before we can solve a behavioral problem, we must first attempt to understand it. What does it mean? What purpose does it serve? What message does it attempt to convey?

A good assessment is like a newspaper article. It asks the questions: Who? What? When? Where? and Why? and provides an organized framework for finding the answers to those questions. It allows us to gain a shared vision of the problem, and, in the process, often unearths some valuable clues about how to resolve it.

If there is one secret to creating long-lasting behavioral change for persons with special needs, it is to *listen* to those who know the person best. For that reason, this assessment is designed as a series of team discussion questions that seek to find answers within the collective observations, insights, and experiences of the person's team.

One of the many things that we have learned from listening to our teams, is that it is not unusual for families of students with special needs to be a little uncomfortable with the *very word* "behavior", often for good reason, and often because it has been used in the past to label or to limit their son or daughter.

For that reason, we offer an alternative way of thinking about and talking about a person's behavior, that of being merely *signals* of his or her anxiety, difficulty, or distress (stress signals and distress signals). We have found that this small change in wording can go a long way toward making teams feel more comfortable, thereby opening new and unexpected avenues for discussion and problem-solving.

Because some teams prefer the more traditional behavioral language, we offer both options (questions #1 and #2) and allow the team to choose either or both. Whichever path the team selects, the process unfolds in the same way.

I. Areas of Need or Difficulty

(The Stress & Behavior Profile)

1. **Specific Behaviors, Problems, or Concerns**: Describe any specific behaviors, problems, or concerns that the team would like to address:

2. **Stress Signals & Distress Signals**: Describe any early signs or signals that the student may be experiencing anxiety, difficulty, or distress. How does the student *show* his or her stress?

3. **Situations Most Likely:** In what situations is the student's behavior (or stress) *most likely* to occur?

4. **Situations Least Likely**: In what situations is the student's behavior (or stress) *least likely* to occur?

5. **Message & Purpose:** What message or purpose does the student appear to be trying to express or achieve through his or her behavior (or stress signals)? What might he or she be trying to *tell us*?

6. **Medical & Physical**: Are there any medical or physical needs that may underlie or complicate the student's behavior (or stress level)?

7. **Sensory Needs & Stressors**: Are there any sensory-related variables that may underlie or complicate the student's behavior (or stress level)?

8. **Past Strategies**: What strategies have been used in the past to try to prevent or address the student's behavior (or to alleviate his or her anxiety, difficulty, or distress)?

1. Specific Behaviors, Problems, or Concerns

Everything should be made as simple as possible, but not simpler - Albert Einstein

A person's behavior can be a form of self-advocacy, a cry for help, or a language unto itself, but at its core, it is simply an action. As such, it should be able to be described clearly and simply, without judgment or interpretation, in ways that can be recognized and recorded in the same way, at the same time, by different people.

Let's take, for example, Roger, a student whose team described his behavior as "losing his temper". At the end of the semester, one teacher, Margaret, had Roger losing his temper up to five times per day, while another, Barry, almost not at all. Was Roger really so much better for Barry than for Margaret? No, in fact, it was quite the opposite. But Margaret and Barry were defining "losing his temper" differently. One was recording every little foot stomp or grumble, while the other recorded only major blowups.

After only a few minutes of discussion, Margaret and Barry were able to agree that, when Roger loses his temper, he either *throws* something (whatever is nearby), tries to *break* something (usually something of his own, like his I-pad), or *hits* someone (usually whoever was trying to help him). All three of those actions can be easily observed and measured. The team could choose to record each behavior individually or they could keep them together as a functional definition of "losing his temper."

The following worksheet provides a list of some *general* areas of need or difficulty for which the team can add their own *specific*, observable, and measurable behaviors (actions and interactions) as examples of that need or as evidence of that difficulty.

In the end, Roger's team defined his behavior this way: "Roger can sometimes have difficulty in the area of Emotional Regulation (losing his temper), as evidenced by throwing something, breaking something, or hitting someone."

1. Specific Behaviors or Concerns: Describe any behaviors, problems, or concerns that the team would like to address:

☐ **A. General Areas of Need or Difficulty:**

☐ 1. *Emotional Regulation*: Handling anxiety, frustration, disappointment, or other strong emotions.

☐ 2. *Participation & Cooperation*: Following directions, accepting correction, or respecting limits, rules, and boundaries.

☐ 3. *Communication & Self Advocacy*: Expressing wants, needs, feelings, and opinions in respectful and effective ways.

☐ 4. *Social & Interpersonal Interaction*: Interacting with others in respectful and effective ways.

☐ 5. *Other*

☐ **B. Specific Behaviors or Concerns (stated in observable, measurable terms)**

	Specific behavior or concern	Frequency (Per day, week, month, or year)
1		
2		
3		
4		

2. Stress Signals & Distress Signals

Red sky at night, sailors' delight. Red sky in the morning, sailors take warning. – Old Adage

It's a typical morning. Everything is going smoothly. You get up at your usual time. The weather is clear. Traffic is light. You stop for a cup of coffee at your usual place before heading to work. You reach into your pocket or purse and... nothing! Your wallet is gone! Where is it? You think about all the things that are in your wallet: your money, your license, your credit cards. You retrace your steps. You search all the usual spots - Nothing!

When we experience stress, our behavior tends to change in subtle or sometimes dramatic ways. Our breathing might become more shallow, our voices louder, our posture more rigid, and our thoughts less rational. We might even say or do things that we don't really mean and that we will regret later. These are our *stress signals* and *distress signals*, and the more stressed *we* become, the more intense *they* become.

Let's take Sarah, for example, a student who, when stressed, would first become very quiet, then put her head down on her desk and then pull the hood of her sweatshirt up and over her eyes. At such times, if anyone said anything to Sarah, tensions could escalate quickly. However, her team found that if they simply waited patiently until Sarah herself initiated some kind of contact, she almost always came around on her own.

Much like the sailor who observes a red sky in the morning, Sarah's team learned that if they could recognize her early stress signals *before* they became distress signals, they stood a far better chance of helping her to navigate her way back to calm waters.

Note: Some teams have chosen to begin the team process with this question, rather than with a discussion of the student's specific behaviors of concern (skipping question #1 entirely or perhaps reserving it for later). The choice is yours. The process is designed to work just the same, either way.

2. Stress Signals & Distress Signals: Describe any early signs or signals that the student may be experiencing anxiety, difficulty, or distress. How does the student *show* his or her stress or distress?

	Stress Levels	Descriptors
1	**Calm**: Use this level to describe the student *at his or her best* (or least stressed).	a. b. c.
2	**Stress Signals**: Use this level to describe any *early or mild* signals that the student may be experiencing anxiety, difficulty or stress.	a. b. c.
3	**Distress Signals**: Use this level to describe any *later or more advanced* signals that the student may be experiencing anxiety, difficulty, or distress.	a. b. c.
4	**Advanced Distress Signals**: Reserve this level for actions and interactions that are *harmful* to self or others.	a. b. c.

3. Situations Most Likely

The real journey of discovery is not in seeing new lands, but in seeing with new eyes. - M. Proust

The situations in which a behavior occurs can tell us a lot about its message, its purpose, and its meaning. We might find, for example, that a certain behavior (or stress signal) generally occurs in a particular *place*, during a particular *activity*, or at a particular *time* of a day. We can then ask ourselves, "What is it about these situations that make them so stressful or unsuccessful?"

Let's take, for example, Joey, a student who was "acting out" *late in the day*, during *Art Class*, when his *favorite staff person* was on break. Joey's team saw each of these variables as potentially important clues, and so they set about eliminating them one at a time. They moved Joey's Art Class to another period. They re-scheduled his favorite staff person's break time. They even provided him with a rest period and a small snack near the end of the day, just in case he was getting tired or hungry. But *nothing changed*.

Then, one day, for no particular reason, Joey's teacher forgot to open the classroom blinds in the morning. Nobody seemed to really notice or care, and so the blinds remained closed all day. Amazingly, the behavior *did not* occur. The next day, they tried the same thing, but this time on purpose. Same result! The next day, too.

What was actually going on with Joey? Any guesses? Well, as it turned out, Joey viewed the arrival of the first school bus (which he saw through his classroom window) as his cue that it was time to go home. When that didn't happen (because the dismissal was still almost an hour away), he would become increasingly frustrated and angry. But with the blinds closed, Joey did not get his cue, and therefore, did not get upset. Eventually, the team found better ways to help Joey to understand when it was time to go home (which involved a picture schedule, a visual timer, and a very predictable end-of-the-day routine).

Just as in any good mystery, some of the clues in Joey's story were important and some were red herrings. It took a good detective (or in this case a team of them) to figure out which was which.

3. **Situations Most Likely**: In what situations is the student's behavior (or stress) most likely to occur?

☐ A. Within particular **activities, classes, or jobs**:

☐ B. During particular **times** of day, week, month, or year:

☐ C. Within particular **places or environments**:

☐ D. During **transitions** from one activity or location to another:

☐ E. When needing to **wait** for activities to become available (or to end):

☐ F. If a request is **delayed or denied**:

☐ G. If feeling **rushed**:

☐ H. If encountering unexpected **changes** in expectations or routines:

☐ I. In response to **directions or corrections** (being asked to *do* something, to *stop* doing something, or to do something *differently*):

☐ J. In response to **sensory** stimuli (sight, sound, touch, tastes, or movement):

☐ K. Within **food-related** activities or situations:

☐ L. Within **social or interpersonal** situations:

☐ M. When experiencing **illness, discomfort, or fatigue**:

☐ N. **Other**:

4. Situations Least Likely

There is no way to happiness, happiness is the way. -Thich Nhat Hanh

The situations in which a student's behavior (or stress) does *not* occur are just as important to examine as those in which it *does*. We might, for example, find that the problem rarely, if ever, occurs with a particular staff person, or at a particular time of day, during a particular class, or at a particular job. Why?

What is it about these situations that make them less stressful or more successful? How do they differ from the situations in which the problem *does* occur? What can we learn from them? What clues do they offer?

By examining these situations, comparing them with each other, and contrasting them with the problematic situations, we can sometimes begin to see the broad outlines of eventual success.

After all, these are the kinds of activities, places, and situations in which the student is already thriving, happy, and at ease, in which problems rarely if ever occur, and incidentally, in which we as parents and professionals are already doing something right!

4. Situations Least Likely: In what situations is the student's behavior (or stress) *least likely* to occur?

☐ A. Within particular **places or locations** (within the school, home, or community):

☐ B. Within particular times of the **day, week, month, or year**:

☐ C. With particular **people** (family members, staff, friends)

☐ D. Within particular **activities, subjects, or classes**:

   ☐ 1. Computer-related activities (Apps, games, email, social media, websites, etc.):

   ☐ 2. Academic subjects, classes, or skill areas (math, science, history, etc.):

   ☐ 3. Vocational activities or Jobs (or types of jobs):

   ☐ 4. Fitness activities (walking, swimming, shooting baskets, etc.):

   ☐ 5. Leisure activities (art, craft, music, games, etc.):

   ☐ 6. Food-related activities (meals, snacks, cooking class, restaurants, etc.):

☐ E. **Other**:

5. Message & Purpose

The primary motivation in life is to belong and contribute. - Alfred Adler

A person's behavior speaks a variety of messages and seeks a variety of purposes. It says (and sometimes shouts) "I want," "I don't want," "I don't understand," "I'm worried," "I'm confused," "I'm hungry," "I'm angry," "I'm excited," 'I'm tired," or "I'm scared." But it expresses these important messages in ways that push away the very things that it hopes to attract.

Most of us have had the experience at one time or another of using our "behavior" to say something that we should have said with our words. Maybe we gave someone the silent treatment. Maybe we slammed the door on our way out of the house. Maybe we yelled at someone for something that we didn't even care about - all the while hoping that the intended recipient would read our minds and fix the real (but unstated) problem. If you have done any of these things yourself, then you probably have a high degree of empathy for individuals with special needs, who might find themselves in that exact same situation, but who might not actually *have* the right words or the right way to express their true intent.

To the extent that we can figure out what message or purpose our students might be trying to express or achieve through their behavior (or stress signals), we stand a far better chance of helping them to find more respectful and effective ways of expressing that same message or achieving that same purpose.

Of course, we cannot always give our students what they want, even if they ask for it nicely. After all, what they want might not be in their best interest, might not be in the family budget, or might not even be legal; however, we *can* always grant every student the dignity of being listened to, being heard, and of having their thoughts and feelings acknowledged.

Because the field of language and communication is so complex, it is important to have someone skilled in that area (Speech Therapist, Communications Disorders Specialist, Autism Specialist, etc.) as part of the team.

5. Message & Purpose: What message or purpose does the student appear to be trying to express or achieve through his or her behavior (or stress signals)? What might he or she be trying to *tell* us?

☐ A. To **refuse, postpone, end or interrupt** unwanted or stressful activities or interactions:

☐ B. To **gain access** to desired items or activities (to request or to add emphasis to a request):

☐ C. To gain **attention, reaction, recognition, or respect**:

☐ D. To initiate or maintain a **social** interaction:

☐ E. To express **confusion** with an activity, situation, or request:

☐ F. To gain **assistance** or to elicit **help**:

☐ G. To express anxiety, frustration, disappointment, or other **strong emotions**:

☐ H. To express **illness, discomfort, or fatigue**:

☐ I. To seek or avoid **sensory** input (touch, taste, sight, sound, smell, and movement):

☐ J. **Other**:

6. Medical & Physical

First, do no harm! - The Hippocratic Oath

I f you are like most people, you probably don't *do* your best when you don't *feel* your best.

Many common ailments such as toothaches, stomachaches, headaches, back pain, allergies, and sleep issues can all masquerade as behavioral problems, leaving a person feeling emotionally vulnerable and unable to adequately cope with the challenges of their day.

If we are not feeling well, we might not have the energy to do our jobs, keep up our appearance, or maintain a kind and respectful demeanor. We might have a shorter fuse when dealing with seemingly minor frustrations, and we might even "snap" (react sharply) at the very people who are trying to help us.

This fact can be especially true for someone with special needs, who might be dealing with complex, long-term, or ongoing physical and medical conditions, but who might not be able to fully understand or explain *what's wrong, where it hurts,* or *how to ask for help.*

Gaining an understanding of our students' medical and physical challenges not only helps us to better meet their needs, but also provides a degree of empathy for their struggles, and a more sympathetic and respectful approach to their behavior.

When discussing a student's medical and physical needs, it is important to have a medical expert (such as the school nurse) as a part of the team and to always be respectful of the student's privacy when sharing information.

6. Medical & Physical Needs: Are there any medical or physical needs or issues that may underlie or complicate the student's behavior (or stress level)?

☐ A. **Headaches**:

☐ B. **Toothache**s (or other dental issues)

☐ C. **Stomach aches** (or other digestive problems):

☐ D. **Allergies** (seasonal allergies, food allergies, etc.):

☐ E. **Infections** (ear, nose, throat, etc.):

☐ F. **Pain** issues:

☐ G. **Seizure or neurological** issues:

☐ H. **Physical** impairments or limitations:_

☐ I. **Vision** impairments or limitations:

☐ J. **Hearing** impairments or limitations:

☐ K. **Other**:

7. Sensory Needs & Stressors

We do not see things as they are. We see things as we are. - Anais Nin

We experience our world, first and foremost, through our senses (sight, sound, touch, taste, smell, and movement). Sensory input calms us down, keeps us alert, and helps us to focus on what is important. It also entertains and enlightens us. Literally, thousands of years of exploration and discovery have gone into the development of elaborate forms of sensory stimulation such as art, music, sports, foods, and fashion.

Think for a moment of all the little sensory experiences that make up your day, and how they make you feel: A brisk walk on a crisp Autumn day, sleeping under a heavy blanket on a cold night, warm towels fresh from the dryer, or the smell of bread baking in the oven.

However, if our sensory systems are not functioning in a typical way, those same sights, sounds, touches, tastes, and movements can become a confusing array of mixed messages.

Now, think for a moment of a time when you were in an important meeting and, suddenly, you got a tickle in your throat or an itch that you could not reach. What effect did it have on you? On your anxiety level? On your concentration? And that is just one very small example. For students with sensory processing issues, that effect can be magnified drastically. The tag on the back of their shirt might feel like sandpaper, the sound of a fire alarm might be more painful than a dentist's drill, or the fluorescent lights in their classroom might pulse with the intensity of a searchlight.

Let's take the example of three different students from the same classroom, John, Billy, and Rene. John loved to swing in the school playground. He would swing all day if you let him, and the more he swung the calmer he got. Billy also loved to swing, but if allowed to swing for more than just a few minutes, he got over-stimulated and agitated. Rene got so dizzy and disoriented on the swing that she feared going anywhere near it. *Same exact* swing, three *completely different* responses.

The world of sensory processing is so complex that if your student struggles with such issues, you will want to have an expert (an Occupational Therapist, Physical Therapist, Autism Specialist, etc.) on your team.

7. Sensory Needs or Stressors: Are there any sensory-related variables that may underlie or complicate the student's behavior or stress level? (Include: under-sensitivity, over-sensitivity, sensory-seeking, and sensory-avoidance.)

☐ 1. Sensitivity to **touch** or being touched

☐ 2. Sensitivity to the taste or texture of **foods** (salty, spicy, sweet, sour, crunchy, sticky, messy, etc.)

☐ 3. Sensitivity to the fit or feel of **clothing** (the tags, seams, fabric, tightness, etc.)

☐ 4. Sensitivity to the texture or feel of instructional, vocational, or grooming **materials** (wet, messy, dirty, rough, smooth, etc.)

☐ 5. Sensitivity to **heat, cold, or pain** (under or over sensitivity)

☐ 6. Sensitivity to loud or unexpected **noises**, background noise, crowd noise, fire alarms, certain tones of voice, etc.

☐ 7. Sensitivity to the **smell or scent** of perfumes, cleaning supplies, foods, etc.

☐ 8. Sensitivity to **visual stimulation** (lighting, motion, distraction, color, etc.)

☐ 9. Sensitivity to **motion and movement** (walking, running, riding, rocking, bouncing, twirling, spinning, swinging, etc.)

☐ 10. **Other:**

8. Past Strategies ("What Works?")

Creativity is the freedom to make mistakes. Art is knowing which mistakes to keep. - Scott Adams

The last question of our assessment section explores those strategies that have been used in the past to prevent or address the student's behavior (or to alleviate his or her stress). Its intention is to capture the strategies that have *worked* (even if only sometimes or in part), as well as those that have *not worked* (or maybe even made matters worse). We can learn a lot from both.

To understand how, consider the example of Clark, a 20-year-old student who had struggled with severe self-injury (hitting his own head with his fist) for most of his life. The meaning and purpose of Clark's behavior were a mystery to everyone who knew and loved him, and in fact, over the years, it had probably taken on so many meanings, and served so many purposes, that they would now be difficult to untangle.

Clark's teacher, Kay, noticed that Clark often wrapped his hand tightly in his own shirt as if trying to self-restrain. She also noticed that he often wore a tight elastic wristband that he pulled snugly over his hand and fingers, and that he seemed calmer when he was wearing it. Kay wondered if the tight wristband, or something like it, might possibly hold the answer to Clark's self-injury.

The next morning, Kay shared her observations in our team meeting, and an Occupational Therapist recognized what she thought might be a need for something called "proprioceptive input" - the kind of sensory input that you get from a heavy blanket, a deep hug, a *tight wristband*, or maybe even from certain kinds of self-injury. A lightbulb seemed to turn on above her head.

Well, as it turned out, the wristband was *not* the solution to Clark's problem, but it was the clue that led to the development of a comprehensive sensory program that was embedded throughout Clark's entire day, and which *did* turn out to be the solution.

8. Past Strategies: What strategies have been used in the past to try to prevent or address the student's behavior (or to alleviate his or her anxiety, difficulty, or distress)?

What Works? *At least sometimes or in part?*	**What Doesn't Work?** *Or maybe even makes matters worse?*

Section II

Success Strategies

Section II

❖

Success Strategies

There are but three things to happiness: something to do, someone to love, and something to look forward to.
- Immanuel Kant

We first saw this quote posted on a classroom bulletin board several years ago. Its message is simple: that we really only need a few basic things in order to be happy. This section of our process focuses on seeing if we can figure out what those few, basic things might be for the person who is at the heart of our discussion.

The strategies discussed in this section are designed to *increase* the likelihood of a student's success, and thereby make behaviors, problems, and stressors *less likely* to occur.

Each strategy springs directly from the information gathered during our assessment (section I), and each is presented in terms of basic everyday human needs - the kinds of things that we *all* need in order to be happy, calm, and successful:

- Strengths & Interests
- Adaptations & Supports
- Space & Environment
- Time & Schedule
- Clear & Visual Information
- Choice & Options
- Communication & Self Advocacy
- Attention, Recognition & Respect
- Limits & Boundaries
- Rewards & Incentives

As in our assessment, this section employs a one-page set of preventive and educative strategies (like tools in a toolbox) with each strategy corresponding to its own one-page supplemental checklist (strategy #1 corresponds to checklist #1).

II. Success Strategies

1. **Strengths & Interests**: Use the student's own strengths and interests to create meaningful and motivating instructional, vocational, and leisure activities.

2. **Adaptations & Supports**: Eliminate, modify, or adapt predictably problematic activities toward clarity, simplicity, and success.

3. **Space & Environment**: Adapt the physical environment in ways that increase the student's likelihood of success, and which make his or her behaviors (or stressors) less likely to occur.

4. **Time & Schedule**: Help the student to better understand the pace, flow, and structure of his or her day (through predictable routines, schedules, time-keeping tools, etc.)

5. **Clear & Visual Information**: Provide information in the form and manner most likely to be easily understood and well received.

6. **Choices & Options**: Involve the student more fully in the plans and decisions of his or her daily life.

7. **Communication & Self Advocacy**: Help the student to express wants, needs, feelings, and opinions in more respectful and effective ways.

8. **Attention, Recognition & Respect**: Teach the student how to get attention, recognition, and respect in respectful and effective ways.

9. **Limits, Rules, & Boundaries**: Provide clear and fair limits, rules, and boundaries based upon safety and respect (not just compliance).

10. **Reward & Incentive**: Reinforce (support) the student's efforts at participation, cooperation, and self-control.

1. Strengths & Interests

Notice the things that bring you joy, the things that make time pass quickly and effortlessly. These are the keys to your path. - Wayne Dyer

We all know people who can immerse themselves for hours on end in their garden, on their computer, or within the pages of a good book.

Similarly, we all have certain activities that seem to come naturally to us, that we accomplish with little or no effort, and during which time seems to fly.

And we can all think of things that we have done *freely* for family or friends that no one else could have *paid* us enough to do.

We do these things, without thought of payment or reward, because we *love* what we are doing, because we love the *people* that we are doing them for, or because we have a *"knack"* for the skills involved.

To the extent that our work, our play, and our learning are based upon our own strengths and interests, we tend to be happier, healthier, and more successful. And when it comes to finding our direction in life, our strengths and interests can be like a compass pointing true north.

As with practically everything else, success is often "all in the details". So, when answering this question, try to be as specific as possible. Don't say, for example, "Brad likes music", but rather, "Brad likes British rock bands of the 1960s and early 1970s" (more on Brad, later). You just never know where the key to success might be hiding.

Note: Some teams have chosen to begin the entire process with this question, rather than with a discussion of the student's specific behaviors of concern (or stress signals), in order to get the discussion started in a positive direction, and to put the student's behavior (or stress) into its proper perspective as being just one small part of who he or she is. Parents generally like this option, students prefer it, and teachers appreciate being able to show off their students' strengths and interests before discussing any potentially delicate issues.

1. Strengths & Interests: Use the student's own strengths and interests to create meaningful and motivating academic, vocational, and leisure activities

- [ ] A. Favorite **computer** sites, programs, Apps, games, social media, websites, etc.

- [ ] B. Favorite **music**, types of music, musical artists, songs, radio stations, instruments, etc.

- [ ] C. Favorite **visual media** (TV shows, movies, videos, etc.)

- [ ] D. Favorite **reading material** (specific books, magazines, newspapers, websites, etc.)

- [ ] E. Favorite **academic** subjects, classes, or skill areas (math, science, history, etc.)

- [ ] F. Favorite **toys and games** (specific board games, card games, electronic games, etc.)

- [ ] G. Favorite **Art/Craft** activities (drawing, painting, coloring, tracing, craft projects.)

- [ ] H. Favorite **fitness** activities (walking, swimming, shooting baskets, etc.)

- [ ] I. Favorite **community** sites (stores, restaurants, parks, libraries, etc.)

- [ ] J. Favorite **foods and beverages** (fruits, vegetables, meats, snacks, drinks, etc.)

- [ ] K. Favorite **vocational jobs** (active, mobile, physical, hands-on, organizational, service-related, office-related, etc.)

- [ ] L. **Special abilities**, skills, talents, hobbies, or intense interests

- [ ] M. **Special qualities** (kindness, humor, honesty, determination, friendliness, sociability, helpfulness, etc.)

- [ ] N. **Other:**

2. Adaptations & Supports

For me, there are only two types of learning, the easy and the impossible -Temple Grandin

Just as we all have our own unique strengths and interests, so too, do we all have our own particular dis-interests and difficulties: skills that we can never seem to master no matter how hard we try, classes in which we continually struggle to pay attention (or to stay awake), and situations in which time seems to crawl at a snail's pace. Whether it is dealing with a temperamental computer, cleaning the house, or handling an uncomfortable social situation, we all have *something*! Nobody is good at everything.

These might also be the kinds of situations in which we tend to experience anxiety, difficulty, or distress, and in which we might sometimes lose our temper or act in ways that we later regret. That can be especially true for individuals with special needs, who might not always be able to tell us what's *wrong*, what they *feel,* or what they *need*.

And of course, the activities that cause a person difficulty are not always the ones that they dislike. Some-times, even a person's favorite activities can get them into trouble. Take, for example, Henry, a student who loved video games so much that he stayed up all night playing them (which caused problems the next day at school.) Or Jill, whose love of social media created all kinds of drama in her life (which she also loved, but which was definitely *not* helpful).

How we address such predictably problematic activities is a team decision. We might, for example, decide to *eliminate* an activity entirely (at least for a while, especially if it serves no immediate or important purpose). Or we might decide to try to *adapt* it toward *clarity, simplicity, and success*.

The worksheet for this strategy lists several easy and practical adaptations and supports that the team might consider in their attempt to make a particular activity less stressful and more successful.

2. Adaptations & Supports: Eliminate, modify, or adapt predictably problematic activities toward *clarity, simplicity, and success.*

- [ ] A. **Identify** the specific activities that cause the student anxiety, difficulty, or distress (academic, vocational, domestic, leisure, social, etc.).

- [ ] B. **Eliminate** predictably problematic activities that serve no immediate or important purpose (at least temporarily).

- [ ] C. **Replace** problematic low-interest activities with higher-interest ones of the same type or purpose (e. g. switching one type of fitness activity for another).

- [ ] D. **Adapt** activities, materials, and curriculum toward clarity, simplicity, and success (make them easier to hold, handle, see, hear, manipulate, or accomplish).

- [ ] E. **Present** the activity through the student's best learning style (visual, auditory, hands-on, interactive, social, etc.).

- [ ] F. **Reduce** expectations until finding the student's level of *confident success* (the amount of work, the number of steps, the length of time, or the level of difficulty).

- [ ] G. **Increase** the durability, stability, and safety of materials and equipment (bolster, brace, strengthen, cushion, anchor down, etc.).

- [ ] H. **Put Away** unwanted distractions and temptations (out of sight and out of reach).

- [ ] I. **Minimize** sensory stressors (sights, sounds, touch, tastes, or movements).

- [ ] J. **Other:**

3. Space & Environment

Change your surroundings, change your life!

The physical space in which an activity occurs can have a profound effect on the behavior of those within it. Think of a gymnasium, a library, a church, a doctor's waiting room, a factory work floor, or a computer lab. Each setting wordlessly suggests the noise level, activity level, and type of interactions that will (and will not) occur within it.

We all have certain places in which we just seem to feel more comfortable, organized, and at ease; and others in which we simply cannot seem to function at all. And we all have our own differing needs for personal space - the amount of space surrounding us, within which we feel safe and calm (and without which we feel anxious and maybe even a little bit threatened).

If we can learn to adapt the physical environment in ways that provide both the *amount* and the *type* of space that a student needs, we can often increase his or her likelihood of success, and make potential problems less likely to occur.

Let's take, for example, Charlie, a student who had difficulty understanding and respecting other people's personal boundaries. If seated around a table with his classmates, Charlie would touch, hug, or lean against whoever was beside him. To complicate matters further, when upset, he would impulsively strike out at anyone who was within arm's reach.

Then, one day, Charlie's teacher happened to observe him sitting in a comfortable easy chair in the school library. She noticed that he seemed more at ease and that he didn't have the same impulse (or ability) to reach out and touch everyone. The chair itself seemed to provide him with the social boundaries that he needed. Charlie's teacher borrowed the chair from the library and placed it near the meeting table in the classroom - close enough to allow Charlie to fully participate, but just far enough away to provide him with some much-needed personal space. It soon became Charlie's favorite place to start his day, get himself organized, and participate in group activities. He even started to seek it out whenever he felt anxious or upset!

Charlie's chair taught him a lot about maintaining good social and personal boundaries, and it never had to say a word! That is an example of the power of space and the environment.

3. Space & Environment: Adapt the physical environment in ways that increase the student's likelihood of success, and that make his or her behaviors (or stressors) less likely to occur.

☐ A. **Setting**: Choose an environment that naturally suits the activity (one that is spacious enough, organized to the purpose, accessible, comfortable, quiet, etc.).

☐ B. **Seating**: Consider seating options that naturally provide good personal boundaries (an easy chair, rocker, recliner, various types of personal desks or group tables, etc.).

☐ C. **Room arrangement**: Use the natural elements of a room (furniture, tables, partitions, etc.) to enhance personal space and to provide subtle personal boundaries (For example, sitting across a table from someone rather than sitting side by side).

☐ D. **"My own space"**: Provide the student with his or her own consistent spot within each primary environment (his or her personal desk, chair, table space, etc.).

☐ E. **Calm space**: Create safe, comfortable, and easily accessible spaces (comfy chair, desk, reading nook, etc.) where students can relax and regroup.

☐ F. **Workspace**: Create distinct and separate areas and "stations" within the room (messy art tables, quiet academic areas, organized workstations, etc.).

☐ G. **Storage space**: Provide a safe place (shelf, drawer, locker, etc.) for the student to store personal or potentially distracting items.

☐ H. **Temptation level:** Put distracting or fragile items out of sight, out of reach, anchored down, or stored away.

☐ I. **Stimulation level**: Reduce the noise, distraction, clutter, and activity level within the environment.

☐ J. **Other**:

4. Time & Schedule

Mommy, how many songs until the church is over?

Time is such an abstract concept, yet one on which we rely in very concrete and practical ways. We want to know how long it will be until payday, until lunch, until an assignment is due, until our vacation, and until our next bathroom break!

And if we do not have access to that information (such as when stuck in a traffic jam on our way to an important meeting), we can become frustrated, anxious, and sometimes even a little "inappropriate".

This effect is magnified for someone who might not have sophisticated time-telling skills, and who must therefore be dependent on others for clues as to how long he or she must wait until desired activities become available or less desired activities will be over.

Time is sometimes called the great healer. It may not literally "heal all wounds," but it certainly does provide us with an opportunity to think, process, reflect, and decide. And the more time we are able to give ourselves (and others), the better those decisions usually turn out to be.

The team's goal here is two-fold: to provide a clear and concrete way for the student to understand the *concept of time*, and also to provide him or her with *enough time* to fully process and respond to the instructions, corrections, transitions, and decisions of his or her daily life.

The list of ways in which we can provide someone with a clear sense of time is practically endless but includes such things as predictable routines, daily rituals, visual schedules, clocks, timers, checklists, and calendars. Or, as one ingenious student asked her mother on a Sunday morning, "*Mommy, how many songs until the church is over?*".

4. Time & Schedule: Help the student to better understand the pace, flow, and structure of his or her day (through predictable routines, schedules, time-keeping tools, etc.).

☐ A. **Processing time**: Provide the student with *enough* time to *fully* process and respond to the instructions, questions, transitions, and decisions of his or her day.

☐ B. **Predictable Routine**: Provide a predictable and reliable routine that allows the student to better *anticipate and prepare* him or herself for upcoming activities and events.

☐ C. **Written or picture schedule**: Create a visual schedule that clearly shows the *structure and sequence* of the student's day (through word, picture, or symbol).

☐ D. **Checklists**: Provide a to-do list of classes, activities, or tasks that can be checked off or crossed through as completed.

☐ E. **First/Then**: Break down the student's schedule into a clear, concise "First this/ Then that" format that simply shows "What I do now" and "What I do next."

☐ F. **Obvious ending points**: Set out the exact amount of work to be completed so that "The end is always in sight" (e.g. Let's do *these* three problems, then we're done.").

☐ G. **Time-keeping tools**: Employ devices that make the time a more *concrete and observable* process (a watch, clock, visual timer, number line, cross-off list, etc.).

☐ H. **Organizational tool**s: Provide a calendar, daily planner, assignment folder, etc. that helps the student to *keep track of* daily, weekly, and monthly events.

☐ I. **Waiting items:** Provide something to *occupy* the student's hands and thoughts while waiting (for example, a magazine, a word-find game, a snack, a song, a video clip, a fidget item, etc.).

☐ J. **Transition items**: Provide something for the student to *carry or deliver* from one activity or place to another (such as an envelope, a box, a note, a joke to tell, etc.).

5. Clear & Visual Information

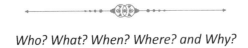

Who? What? When? Where? and Why?

The answers to these five questions not only form the foundation of almost every good news story, but also provide most of the information that we need in order to navigate our way through the day. Consider for example, how you might feel if you were told to attend a training session for your job, but were not given clear information about *who* would be teaching, *what* you would be expected to learn *when* you would be finished, *where* the session was being held, or w*hy* you were being asked to attend? Not knowing the answer to any one of those five questions would be enough to make most people anxious.

Information is inherently calming, but to serve its purpose, it must be delivered in a way that matches the learning style of the person who is meant to receive and act upon it.

Verbal language, for example, can be a great source of information for someone who is an auditory learner, but it can also be a tangled web of subtle nuances, unspoken inferences, and confusing figures of speech. Plus, it disappears into thin air as it is spoken. It is not unusual for individuals with special needs to have difficulty processing verbal information, and that difficulty can increase, sometimes dramatically, if they are already feeling anxious.

Visual information, on the other hand, tends to be easier to remember, and it remains available for future reference. A simple visual image can instantly evoke a clear and indelible message. Just think of the American flag, the Golden Arches, or a traffic stop sign.

A picture is worth a thousand words, in part because it crosses language barriers and bypasses the need for auditory processing. People who speak different languages can look at a picture and pretty much interpret it in the same way. No translator is needed!

Regardless of which way we choose to deliver information, the point is the same - to be clear in our meaning and concise in our delivery so that the person always knows *who, what, when, where, and why* they are being asked to do what they are doing.

5. Clear & Visual Information: Provide information in the form and manner most likely to be easily understood and well received.

☐ A. **Who?** Make sure that the student knows who he or she can turn to for information or support in every situation.

☐ B. **What?** Make sure that the student knows what he or she is supposed to do and how to do it.

☐ C. **When?** Make sure that the student understands his or her schedule (What do I do now? When will I be finished? What comes next? When is my break? When is lunch?).

☐ D. **Where?** Make sure that the student knows where he or she is supposed to be, where to find materials, and where to go if needing a break.

☐ E. **Why?** Make sure that the student knows why he or she is being asked to do something.

☐ F. **Be Positive**: Let the student know what to *do* rather than what *not* to do (for example, "Stay with me" rather than "Don't run" or "Gentle hands" rather than "Don't hit").

☐ G. **Be Clear & Concise**: Reduce the *length and complexity* of our words. Refrain from humor, metaphors, or slang that might be difficult for the student to interpret.

☐ H. **Be more visual, less verbal**: Present directions, choices, questions, recipes, menus, and schedules through visual rather than purely verbal means:

   ☐ 1. Picture, Photo, or Symbol:

   ☐ 2. Gesture or Sign:

   ☐ 3. Demonstration, Modeling, or Observation:

   ☐ 4. Bins or Templates (to help count or sort):

   ☐ 5. Written Directions, Post-it Notes, Checklists:

   ☐ 6. Video clips, tutorial films, educational games, and web sites:

   ☐ 7. Finished models (to copy and replicate):

   ☐ 8. Other:

6. Choice & Options

If you can't make up your mind about something, flip a coin. You'll know what you want before the coin hits the floor. -Unknown

We all like to have some say in the plans and decisions of our daily lives. We don't like to be told answers, we like to discover them for ourselves. And we hate it when others try to force or manipulate us into doing something against our will, even if we secretly know that it is in our best interest or for our own good.

As adults, we often *gravitate* toward the things that we do well, *prioritize* what we think is important, and *artfully dodge* much of the rest of it. Our students do that too, but they might need our help to do so in safe, respectful, and effective ways.

It is not unusual for students with special needs to find themselves in situations in which many, if not most, of the decisions in their day, are controlled by others, from when they get up in the morning, to what they eat, to where they go to school or work. For them, every opportunity to make a choice, even a small choice, is an important one (and every small choice is good practice for the bigger decisions that will inevitably come along.).

Choices and options can make a person feel *empowered*, valued, and respected, but they can also be *stressful*. And, much like all the other variables we are discussing, decision-making is often a very personal thing.

For example, some of us find it easier to make a choice if our options are offered one at a time (to be either rejected or accepted). Some of us are able to handle two choices (but no more than that). Some of us need our choices to be displayed visually (through pictures, a written list, or a menu). Some of us need extensive time to ponder our options (maybe seconds, maybe minutes, maybe hours, or maybe even days). We are all different.

And of course, there are times in our lives when we just want somebody else (somebody we trust) to make the decision for us. And yes, that is also a decision!

6. Choices & Options: Involve the student more fully in the plans and decisions of his or her daily life.

☐ A. **Input into the schedule**: Actively solicit the student's input when planning the activities, jobs, and classes that make up his or her daily and weekly schedule.

☐ B. **Provide** small choices within larger activities: For example, "Where shall we sit?", "What color pen shall we use?", "Which of these two tasks shall we do first?".

☐ C. **Negotiation and compromise**: Be open to a little give and take. Try to find an acceptable alternative to a resisted activity.

☐ D. **Input into goals and objectives**: Encourage student involvement in the creation of goals and objectives (at whatever level he or she can participate).

☐ E. **Present choices in a form and manner** most likely to be easily understood and well received.

☐ F. **Present choices one at a time** (to be either rejected or accepted), **two at a time** (to be chosen between), or as part of a larger **array** (such as a menu).

☐ G. **Present options visually,** through pictures, text, notes, checklists, or actual objects.

☐ H. **Provide easy (and nonverbal) ways for the student to make his or her choice known** (for example, by giving a thumbs up or thumbs down, pointing to what he or she wants, circling a choice on a list or menu, by crossing out unwanted options, etc.

☐ I. **Other:**

7. Communication & Self Advocacy

The greatest desire of the human heart is to be listened to and to be heard - Richard Carlson

Communication is central to the human experience. It's how we let each other know our wants, needs, feelings, and opinions. It's how we share our knowledge and our history. It's how we negotiate and compromise. It's how we connect with each other. It's how we *order Pizza!* And yet, for some reason, saying the things that we most want to say to each other is not always easy.

Take, for example, a student, let's call him Mike, who returned to his classroom red-faced and angry, following an end-of-the-school-year luncheon, insisting that his support staff, Betty, deliberately ate his hamburger! As it turned out, the waitress mistakenly gave Mike's hamburger (with extra pickles) to Betty, and she took a bite before realizing the problem.

Over the course of about half an hour, Mike relayed his story to his teacher, who mostly just sat and listened, except for asking an occasional question:

"Did Betty order you another hamburger?" ("Yes, she did.") "Was it good?" ("Yes, it was.")

"Did it have extra pickles?" ("Yes, it did.")

Finally, when Mike seemed to have reached the end of his story, his teacher asked if there was anything else that he wanted to say. Yes, there was. "What is it, Mike?", his teacher asked. *"I'm graduating."* The conversation, which moments before had seemed over, had only just begun.

Later that same week another student, let's call her Maria, entered school in the morning as usual, but then immediately threw a chair against the wall and crawled under a table in the front hallway, refusing to move or speak. Eventually, a trusted staff person was able to coax Maria out from under the table. Her issue? *"I'm graduating."*

Mike and Maria's message was the same, they were both afraid of graduating and of leaving the comfort and security of their school and the people who understood them so well. But they said it through hamburgers and hallway tables.

Our mission is to help *our* Mikes and *our* Marias to express *their* wants, needs, feelings, and opinions in increasingly respectful and effective ways so that their message can be heard and their needs met.

7. Communication & Self Advocacy: Help the student to express his or her wants, needs, feelings, and opinions in more respectful and effective ways.

☐ A. To **refuse, postpone end, or interrupt** unwanted activities or interactions ("No thanks!")

Current strategy:

Possible replacement strategy:

☐ B. To **request or gain access** to desired items or activities ("I want that")

Current strategy:

Possible replacement strategy:

☐ C. To gain **attention, reaction, recognition, or respect** ("Pay attention to me!")

Current strategy:

Possible replacement strategy:

☐ D. To initiate or maintain a **social** interaction ("Hi", "How's it going?")

Current strategy:

Possible replacement strategy:

☐ E. To express **confusion** with directions or expectations ("I don't understand.")

Current strategy:

Possible replacement strategy:

☐ F. To express anxiety, frustration, anger, or other **strong emotions** ("I'm upset!")

Current strategy:

Possible replacement strategy:

☐ G. To express **illness, discomfort, or fatigue** ("I don't feel well.")

Current strategy:

Possible replacement strategy:

☐ H. **Other:**

8. Attention, Recognition & Respect

Give value, and give nothing else - Dr. John McGee

Our attention (what we notice and where we focus) is perhaps the simplest yet most powerful tool in our toolbox. Consider, for example, how our behavior changes in subtle or dramatic ways when we sense that we are being observed (perhaps by a supervisor, or by someone that we want to impress). Without even knowing it, we tend to "put our best foot forward" and make slight adjustments in our posture, our attitude, and our actions.

Certain behaviors are sometimes said to be "attention-getting" because they seem intended to elicit a response or reaction from others. However, seeking attention is not inherently a bad thing. It is a basic human need that we all share. The real problem, for our students, is often that their methods of attention-seeking may not always be *subtle enough*, *clear enough*, or *respectful enough* to be received in the way intended.

The author Richard Carlson has written that "the greatest desire of the human heart is to be listened to and to be heard." We all need attention, recognition, and respect. But we may not all know how to get it.

By consciously placing our attention where it will do the most good, we can help our students to learn better ways to get the attention that they desire and deserve.

Attention, recognition, and respect are such basic human needs that they should not have to be earned. Even in the most challenging of situations, we can always find something about a person to affirm and respect. If you are not quite sure what to say, try starting with something like, "*I like the way that you...*". Anything you say after that will probably be okay.

As Dale Carnegie once wrote, "All of us, be we butcher, baker or king, like those who like us," and the same could be said of attention, recognition, and respect.

8. Attention, Recognition & Respect: Teach the student how to get attention, recognition, and respect in more respectful and effective ways.

☐ A. **Ignore or give a low-level response** to actions and interactions that we would like to see a decrease.

☐ B. **Acknowledge, praise, and attend** to those actions and interactions that we would like to see an increase ("I like the way that you...", "I'm so proud of how you...", "That was such a nice thing to do", "I really appreciated it when you...").

☐ C. **Point out the personal qualities** that you appreciate about the student (such as kindness, honesty, respect, determination, friendliness, and helpfulness).

☐ D. **Show the student a better way to get your attention** (raising their hand, tapping you on the shoulder, using a specific phrase, pointing to a specific symbol, etc.) and then be prepared to honor and respond to it.

☐ E. **Give genuine and sincere praise** in the style and manner that the student would appreciate the most. For example, some students love direct and effusive praise, while others prefer more subtle forms of recognition such as a thumbs up, a knuckle bump, or a note placed quietly on their desk.

☐ F. **Other:**

9. Limits, Rules & Boundaries

Treat others as you would like to be treated- The Golden Rule

As much as we might like to think of ourselves as rebels or free spirits, in reality, we all benefit from having clear and fair limits, rules, and boundaries. Far from being a hindrance to our freedom, such restrictions provide us with a sense of predictability and stability that actually "frees us up" from inadvertently making mistakes that might put us in harmful situations, do damage to our reputation, or limit our access to important living and learning opportunities.

Most of us want to know what our limits are, even as we test and protest them, and most of us tend to rebel at a level just above where those limits are set. But to be effective in the long run, limits, rules, and boundaries must spring from a sense of respect for the individual, their peers, and their community (not just compliance).

We once knew a student, let's call him Matt, who had fallen into a pattern of mischievously sitting at his teacher Emily's desk and rifling through her papers. Initially, of course, Emily was extremely frustrated. After all, these were legal documents that she was responsible for.

Eventually, Emily hit upon the simple idea of putting a masking-tape line on the floor to visually separate her desk area from the students' area. She pointed out the line every day to her students and praised them every day for knowing about the line and for respecting it, and for a while, she also made sure that all the papers on her desk were meaningless ones that she didn't need to protect.

Matt initially ignored the tape, of course, but over time, he gradually seemed to get used to it. During week two, he was observed tentatively dipping his toe across the line as if "testing the water". During week three, he was seen actually scolding a classmate who had crossed the line (even though Matt himself was still crossing it regularly). And within a couple more weeks he rarely even went near the teacher's area.

Someone once said that "In the midst of crisis, we tend to overlook the obvious" - in this case, that a clear and simple rule (here, just a piece of masking tape) can sometimes make a big difference in a person's life.

9. Limits, Rules, & Boundaries: Provide clear and fair limits, rules, and boundaries based upon safety and respect (not just compliance).

☐ A. **Safety-based rules**: Define the actions and interactions that cannot be safely accessed or allowed (stove, street, potential weapons, other people's property, etc.).

☐ B. **Situation-specific rules**: Define those activities which can be allowed but only within specific circumstances or with certain restrictions, for example:

☐ By Time ("Snack at 2:00", "Music for 15 minutes")

☐ By Place ("Paint in the art area", "Play ball outside", "Run in the gym")

☐ By Number ("Just one hug", "Two cookies per person")

☐ By Person ("Only with staff", "Only with family")

☐ C. Make rules **more visual/ less verbal**: For example, by placing a masking tape line on the floor (to define a private area), or by placing a big red Stop Sign over a computer screen (when it is not computer time.).

☐ D. **Post** written or pictorial rules in areas where they can be easily seen and referred to.

☐ E. **Review** rules immediately before entering the situation in which they will be needed (for example, review lunchroom rules just before entering the cafeteria).

☐ F. **Respect-based rules:** Make safety and respect (rather than compliance) the foundation for your rules, for example, respectful touch, respectful volume, respectful language, and respect for others' privacy, property, or personal space.

☐ G. Provide students the opportunity to **participate in the creation** of their own rules and give them frequent opportunities to be the ones to share those rules with others.

☐ H. **Other**:

10. Reward & Incentive

Accentuate the positive, eliminate the negative, latch on to the affirmative, and don't mess with Mr. In-between. - Harold Arlen

The dictionary defines the word "reinforce" as meaning "to bolster, brace, and support", as with the girders, beams, and bolts that reinforce a building or a bridge.

A reward (or reinforcer) is a tangible symbol of appreciation and respect - not a bribe, but a fair exchange for an honest effort. It gives us something to look forward to and can serve as a point of genuine connection between the person giving the reward and the one receiving it.

Consider, for example, Martin, a teacher who treated his student, Bobby, to a can of soda after Bobby handled a challenging situation especially well. Was the can of soda a reward? Or did it simply provide Martin with an *opportunity* to show his appreciation to Bobby in a tangible way? Isn't Martin's appreciation the real reward? Just like if we meet a friend for coffee on a Saturday morning. Is the cup of coffee the real reason that we got up early on our day off and drove halfway across town? Probably not, but it's what *got us there*.

We all have times in our lives when we need a little extra incentive to keep us motivated. And we all have times when just having a little *something to look forward to* is enough to get us through a difficult or unpleasant situation.

There are many different kinds of reward systems available on the market today, and many of them are very good. In our experience, the best ones for a person with special needs are the simplest ones, and the ones created by the person's own team.

Rewards and incentives are not for everybody though. Some people find them anxiety-producing rather than motivating. Some people find them almost insulting. That is why the decision should be made at the team level, by those who know the person best, and in collaboration with the student him or herself.

The following checklist provides the team with some basic guidelines for creating a respectful and effective reward plan that is personalized to the particular student and tailored to his or her own needs.

10. **Reward & Incentive**: Reinforce (support) the student's efforts at participation, cooperation, and self-control.

☐ A. **Choose a skill, behavior, or quality** to reinforce:

    ☐ 1. *Communication*: Expressing wants, needs, feelings, and opinions in respectful and effective ways (for example "Using my words").

    ☐ 2. *Cooperation*: Participating in the planned or requested activities of the classroom, job, or home (for example, "Following my schedule" or completing a task).

    ☐ 3. *Respect*: Treating others as you would like to be treated (for example, using respectful language, respectful volume, respectful touch, or respect for the property).

    ☐ 4. *Emotional regulation:* Handling anxiety, frustration, disappointment, and other strong emotions (For example, "Using my calming strategies").

☐ B. **Choose a reward** that is *high interest, low pressure, inexpensive* (or preferably *free*), and *always available* whenever and wherever it is earned. For example

    ☐ 1. *Activities* (playing a game, shooting baskets, coloring, listening to music, etc.)

    ☐ 2. *Items* (trinkets, stickers, certificates of appreciation, etc.)

    ☐ 3. *Time* (time with a friend, extra free time, computer time, etc.)

    ☐ 4. *Snacks* (a can of pop, a few crackers, a stick of gum, a bag of chips, etc.)

    ☐ 5. Special *responsibilities or privileges* (being a leader, helper, attendance taker, etc.)

☐ C. **Choose a criterion for success** that is *attainable* within a reasonable amount of time (for example, upon completing a certain task or a certain number of tasks).

☐ D. Schedule **preferred activities to follow less preferred ones** (so that the person always has "something to look forward to").

☐ E. Use **visual tools** (charts, reward cards, stars, stickers, happy faces, etc.) to clearly show the student his or her progress toward success and reward, e.g. "Three stars on my reward card = computer time".

☐ F. **Other**:

Section III

Calming & Coping Strategies

Section III

Calming & Coping Strategies

You cannot calm the storm. Calm yourself. The storm will pass -Timber Hawkeye

I f we view a student's behavior as being a signal of his or her anxiety, difficulty, or distress, then any successful plan for resolving that behavior, or alleviating that stress, must include a set of reliable calming and coping strategies.

Just as with everything else in life, we all deal with stress in our own unique ways. Some of us seek out the company of friends and family. Others seek out silence and solitude. Some of us "sweat it out" in the gym. Others "sleep it off" on the couch. Some of us turn down the volume on our car radios. Others crank it up. There is no right or wrong way to do it.

All of the Success Strategies discussed in Section II are also Calming and Coping Strategies in that they set the student up for success and thereby lower his or her stress. This section will focus primarily on strategies that help the student to relax and regroup *during* moments of stress.

As with the preceding sections, we provide a *one-page* set of calming and coping strategies, with each strategy corresponding to its own *one-page* supplementary checklist (strategy #1 corresponds to checklist #1).

Each strategy is presented in terms of basic everyday human needs - the kinds of things that we *all* need in order to feel safe and calm.

- Calming Tasks & Activities

- Time & Space

- Exercise & Movement

- Respectful Refusals & Dignified Escapes

- Listening & Acknowledgement

- Rest & Recovery

- Instruction & Practice (Specific Calming Techniques)

- Plan B

III. Calming & Coping Strategies

1. **Calming Tasks & Activities**: Provide a set of predictably calming tasks and activities that help the student to relax and regroup during times of anxiety, difficulty, or distress.

2. **Time & Space**: Provide the student with enough time and space to truly relax and regroup.

3. **Exercise & Movement**: Provide opportunities for the student to release and re-channel his or her excess or nervous energy.

4. **Respectful Refusals & Dignified Escapes**: Teach the student how to respectfully refuse, postpone, end, or interrupt unwanted or stressful activities and interactions.

5. **Listening & Acknowledgement**: Listen supportively, without judgment or interruption, to the student's worries and concerns.

6. **Distraction & Change**: Introduce a new or compelling idea, topic, or activity in order to redirect the student's attention away from his or her worries or concerns.

7. **Rest & Recovery**: Provide opportunities for the student to rest, relax, or sleep.

8. **Instruction & Practice** (Specific Calming Techniques): Teach, model, and practice simple strategies for calming, coping, and managing stress.

9. **Plan B:** Create an alternate schedule or menu of activities that can be used if the student is not ready, willing, or able to participate in the planned activities of his or her day.

1. Calming Tasks & Activities

When I am kind and calm, I live in a kinder, calmer world. -Unknown

We all have certain activities that we instinctively turn to, perhaps without even realizing it, when needing to calm ourselves. We might, for example, clean the house, wash the car, organize the closet, or browse our favorite websites. Such activities have the advantage of being almost automatic, and therefore, of freeing our minds from our worries and concerns.

A few years ago, we participated in a team discussion for a student named Brad, who was struggling with some fairly serious social issues. Brad was new to the school, and his staff hadn't had much of a chance to get to know him yet. During most of the discussion, Brad sat with his head down on the table, clearly not wanting to be there, and silently letting his team answer for him.

When asked about his interests, the team all agreed that Brad seemed to like music. What kind of music? The team wasn't sure. "Maybe children's songs," they said, "maybe oldies."

It was then that Brad finally raised his head (for the first time since he arrived) and said, loudly and clearly, "British rock bands of the 1960s and early 1970s." You could have heard a pin drop! He went on to name "The Beatles," "The Rolling Stones," "The Who," "The Yardbirds," and his personal favorite, "Donovan."

The answer to that one question changed everything for Brad. Music would now fill his life. It was his calming activity during times of stress. It was his conversational ice breaker. It gave him something to do during his free time. And, perhaps most important to our purpose, just bringing up one of Brad's favorite musical groups was often enough to re-direct his attention and re-set his mood.

1. Calming Tasks & Activities: Provide a set of predictably calming tasks and activities that help the student to relax and regroup during times of anxiety, difficulty, or distress.

☐ A. Calming **music** activities: Specific calming songs, artists, stations, or types of music

☐ B. Calming **art/craft** activities: Drawing, coloring, tracing, pasting, etc.

☐ C. Calming **computer** activities: Specific websites, Apps, programs, games, etc.

☐ D. Calming **organizational tasks**: Sorting, matching, filing, making lists, puzzles, etc.

☐ E. Calming **jobs and tasks**: Vocational tasks and household chores have been observed to bring the student a predictable sense of success, accomplishment, and completion.

☐ F. Calming **academic activities**: Familiar and predictably successful worksheets, educational websites, educational games, word finds, etc.

☐ G. Calming **snacks** (or food prep activities): Making, eating, or sharing a piece of toast, a cup of tea, a bowl of popcorn, some crunchy apple slices, a chewy piece of licorice, etc. (Be sure to check for food allergies and issues beforehand).

☐ H. Calming **sensory** activities: Soothing sights, sound, touch, taste, and movements (on the student's own terms, and under the guidance of someone trained in the area of sensory processing).

☐ I. **Other:**

2. Time & Space

Time and Space = Calm and Safe

Time and Space, go together like bread and butter, and when they team up, they might just be the most successful calming and coping combo of all times.

Time is called the "great healer" because it helps us to put some *emotional distance* between ourselves and the source of our frustrations and concerns. It might not literally heal all wounds, but it certainly gives our wounds a chance to heal themselves.

Like time, space is also a powerful healer, in part because it helps us to put some *physical distance* between ourselves and our stressors. It gives us "room to breathe," and keeps us from feeling literally or figuratively "backed into a corner".

The amount of time and space that any of us needs in order to truly recover from a traumatic or emotional experience is highly individualized and can depend on a wide variety of variables, many of which are not within our control.

We cannot necessarily predict how much time or space someone is going to need. Sometimes, we just have to be patient and *wait* quietly until he or she begins showing *signs of readiness*, regardless of how long that might take.

We once knew a student named Sherry who needed lots of time and space (sometimes minutes, sometimes hours) to truly regain her composure after a stressful experience. Her team learned to simply "wait and see". When Sherry finally felt calm enough to reconnect, she would usually come over and silently offer her teacher a stick of gum (or some other such thing). That was her way of letting us know that she was "ready". If her teacher accepted the gum (which she always did), Sherry took it as a sign that all was well (which it usually was).

We cannot always know the right thing to say or do for someone who is in distress (even for someone we know very well), but we can always start by doing them the small-but-great favor of providing a little time and space.

2. Time & Space: Provide the student with enough time and space to truly relax and regroup.

☐ A. **Personal Space**: Provide the student *enough space* to feel truly safe and calm (based upon his or her own observed and perceived needs in similar situations).

☐ B. **Processing time**: Provide the student *enough time* to relax and regroup (quietly and without unsolicited questions, directions, or advice).

☐ C. **"My own space"**: Provide the student with a specific and consistent place in which to relax or take a break (a favorite chair, desk, table, rest area, etc.).

☐ D. **Natural boundaries**: Consider seating options that naturally provide good personal boundaries (an easy chair, rocker, recliner, various types of personal desks, etc.).

☐ E. **Calming places and spaces**: Choose a space that matches the student's own particular calming needs, for example,

　☐ 1. A comfortable *chair* (easy chair, rocker, recliner)

　☐ 2. A *table space* (study carrel, student desk, art table, puzzle table, etc.)

　☐ 3. A *rest* area (with a blanket, pillow, dim lights, etc.)

　☐ 4. An *active* area (gym, etc.) in which to safely expend excess or nervous energy.

　☐ 5. An *activity-based* area (a reading nook, art area, music room, office area, etc.).

　☐ 6. A *quiet* area (away from the source of the student's anxiety, difficulty, or distress)

　☐ 7. A *sensory* area (with access to calming sensory-motor options and support).

　☐ 8. Other:

☐ F. **Signs of readiness**: Wait until the student shows signs of readiness to connect, and a lessening of stress signals, before attempting to re-engage.

☐ G. **Check-ins**: Check in with the student periodically in order to provide an *opportunity* to reconnect, but without pressure to do so ("Just checking in, I'm here if you need me").

☐ H. **Time frame**: Provide a *clear but flexible* time frame for calming (as a guideline, *not* as an expectation) e.g. "Let's relax till the bell rings", "Let's check in after this video is finished", "I'll check back with you in 15 minutes, Okay?", etc.)

☐ G. **Other**:

3. Exercise & Movement

The journey of a thousand miles begins with one step - Lao Tzu

It would be hard to overestimate the benefits that exercise has in our lives. Exercise keeps us healthy, boosts our mood, and gives us energy. It can also be a very powerful calming and coping tool.

Let's take one small example, the simple act of taking a walk:

Taking a walk gets us up and moving, gets our blood flowing, and gives us a chance to release and re-channel our excess or nervous energy.

A walk can provide us with solitude, leaving us alone with our thoughts. Or conversely, it can make us feel less alone, by giving us a chance to interact with people that we pass along the way (even if all we ever say to them is "Hi".)

If we are outside, a walk provides an all-access free pass to the calming beauty of nature.

A walk gives us time to think, and if we are with a trusted person, it can provide an opportunity to talk - but since the point of a walk is the walk itself, talking is optional, and so, nothing to get stressed about.

All these benefits just from taking a walk! Exercise and movement are like that. They calm, energize, and inspire as we stretch, strengthen, and perspire. They are some of our best and truest calming and coping strategies.

3. Exercise & Movement: Provide opportunities for the student to release and re-channel his or her excess of nervous energy.

- [ ] A. **Take a walk**: Locate or create a walking path (or area) outside, inside, around, or within the school, home, yard, gym, or workplace.

- [ ] B. Provide an **errand or delivery** that gets the student up and moving, and which provides a short burst of calming exercise (such as delivering a letter to the office).

- [ ] C. Explore **seating options** that contain an element of subtle movement (such as a rocking chair, an inflated exercise ball, a glider, or a porch swing).

- [ ] D. Provide **short movement breaks** placed strategically throughout the day, in order to catch and release a student's stress before it has a chance to build (a quick stretch, a couple of Yoga poses, a short brisk walk, a chance to dance freely to one song, etc.).

- [ ] E. Provide **sport-related** activities (shooting baskets, playing catch, etc.) that involve exercise and movement.

- [ ] F. Provide access to **safe, open spaces** where the student can safely run around or release his or her energy in non-directed ways (a gym, recess area, fenced-in playground, etc.).

- [ ] G. Explore **online Apps**, videos, and programs that teach exercise and movement-related activities in a fun and informative ways (stretching, calisthenics, yoga, dance, etc.).

- [ ] H. **Other**:

4. Respectful Refusals and Dignified Escape

Just say no. - Nancy Reagan

The right to say "no" is one of the most basic human rights. When we say "no" to someone or to something, we are, in a small way, defining ourselves, declaring our independence, and setting our own personal boundaries.

Many, if not most, inappropriate behaviors occur as an inefficient, though not altogether ineffective, way of saying no to unwanted or feared activities and interactions.

For some people, especially those with a processing delay, saying "no" can also be a valuable way to buy a little extra time to process instructions, questions, and decisions before inadvertently agreeing to something that they do not actually want.

If our students can learn to respectfully refuse, postpone, end, or interrupt unwanted or stressful situations in ways that do not frighten or frustrate others, they stand a far better chance of having their requests honored and their needs met.

And if they can learn how to make a graceful exit from a stressful situation, before their stress signals become distress signals, then they will have learned perhaps the most common, and commonly successful, calming, and coping skill of all - the ability to walk away from trouble.

Obviously, there are times when "opting out" of a situation, even if done nicely, is not a viable option, but we can always at least start the process by honoring the person's "no", and in so doing, honoring the person him or herself, while we try to find our way to "yes."

4. Respectful Refusals & Dignified Escapes: Teach the student how to respectfully refuse, postpone, end, or interrupt unwanted or stressful activities and interactions.

☐ A. Provide the student with the **right words** and the **right way** to refuse, postpone, end, or interrupt unwanted or stressful activities and interactions, for example

   ☐ 1. To refuse ("No thank you")

   ☐ 2. To postpone ("Can I do this later?")

   ☐ 3. To end ("I'm finished")

   ☐ 4. To interrupt ("I need a break")

☐ B. Provide **visual supports** that help the student to express his or her message in clear and effective ways (a picture, symbol, gesture, sign, hall pass, break card, etc.).

☐ C. Provide the student with a **specific and consistent place** in which to take a break (a favorite chair, desk, table, reading nook, sensory area, rest area, etc.).

☐ D. Provide **acceptable alternatives** to a rejected activity so that the student always has an "out" that is acceptable to both teacher and student, or parent and child (an alternate work task, fitness activity, seating option, food choice, etc.).

☐ E. Provide the student with an **errand, mission, or delivery** that gets him or her out of a stressful situation without drawing undue attention to his or her stress or behavior (such as taking an envelope to the office).

☐ F. **Other:**

5. Distraction & Change

In the midst of crisis, we tend to overlook the obvious - T. Bowman

Is it just us, or does it seem like our collective attention span is getting shorter and shorter all the time? Maybe it's due to the fast pace of modern life, or maybe it's because we can access any piece of information or entertainment with the touch of a finger. We seem to get bored so easily, get impatient so quickly, and get distracted by every shiny bauble that comes along.

But there is at least one area of life in which our shortened attention spans can sometimes come in handy, and that is in the area of calming and coping.

We all know people who are naturally good at "letting things go". They just seem to be able to clear their minds, forgive and forget, replace bad thoughts with good, and "move on" to the next opportunity.

But those lucky people are few and far between, and "letting go" is easier said than done. For most of us, it is very difficult to let go of our disappointments and frustrations, even in the best of circumstances, and it can be especially difficult for someone with special needs who might not be able to make the cognitive shift in thinking necessary to get truly "unstuck" from a negative thought or mood.

That is where distraction and change can help. By simply introducing a favorite topic, a compelling idea, a different activity, or a new person into the mix, we can sometimes shift a student's attention away from his or her worries or concerns, and toward a happier, calmer frame of mind. It is a technique that is so simple that we often overlook it.

It's not magic, but it is almost always worth a try.

6. Distraction & Change: Introduce a new or compelling idea, topic, or activity in order to redirect the student's attention away from his or her worries or concerns.

☐ 1.   Change the **topic**: Introduce a new, different, or compelling topic.

☐ 2.   Change the **setting**. Move to a different, calmer, or more comfortable environment.

☐ 3.   Change **staff**: Introduce a new person, someone that the student likes and trusts, or someone who was not part of the stressful situation.

☐ 4.   Change **activities**: Introduce a new, more compelling, or more predictably successful activity.

☐ 5.   Change **peer groupings**: Increase the student's access to people who are naturally calm, cheerful, and resilient. Try to limit access to those who are likely to overreact or contribute to the student's behavior or stress.

☐ 6.   Use **technology**: Take advantage of Smartphone and computer technology to introduce a funny or interesting video clip, song, photo, or idea. Have a few such items always cued up and ready to go.

☐ 7.   Use the student's **strengths and interests** to come up with compelling distractors (topics and activities).

☐ 8.   Let the student **overhear** you talking to someone else about favorite topics, compelling activities, or upcoming events ("Hey Betty, is it true that we are making muffins in Foods Class this afternoon?")

6. Listening & Acknowledgement

People may forget what you say, they may forget what you do, but they will never forget how you made them feel. - Maya Angelo

Dale Carnegie wrote, "Truly listening to someone is the highest compliment that you can give a person." The author Richard Carlson once said "The greatest desire of the human heart is to be listened to and to be heard," and the Psychologist, Carl Rogers, made listening to the cornerstone of his therapeutic approach.

When we truly listen to someone, we let them know that they are important to us, that we value and respect them, and that we take their words and feelings seriously.

We have probably all had the experience of marching into someone's office, intending to confront them over some real or perceived offense, but then having our anger melt away if he or she simply listened to us.

It is not always easy to share our feelings, even with those closest to us, but it is easier if the listener is genuinely interested, and if his or her questions do not pry or judge. Most of us have at least one such person in our lives who we turn to when needing to sort things out, safely vent our frustrations, or make a big decision.

We once worked with a school nurse who had a natural gift for listening. All day long, one after another, students would march into Nurse Pat's office, most complaining of ailments, but many expressing anxiety or distress. Time would pass, and eventually, the door would open and these same students would amble out, calm and serene, wishing Pat a nice day. We once asked Nurse Pat "How the heck do you do that?" To which she replied, "I wear them down with my listening."

Listening serves so many purposes for both the listener and the listened. It respects. It reflects. It informs. It slows things down. It takes the pressure off. It gives everybody time to think. It brings new insights and perspectives. It creates a bond, and it opens the door to problem-solving, negotiation, and compromise.

6. Listening & Acknowledgement: Listen supportively, without judgment or interruption, to the student's worries and concerns.

☐ A. **Have a "Go-To" person**: Make sure that the student always knows who he or she can turn to (and talk to) in every situation.

☐ B. **Regular check-in times**: Schedule routine times for the student to check-in and talk with a trusted person, *before* his or her worries and concerns become "too big".

☐ C. **Listen**: Let the student express his or her worries or concerns fully and freely, without judgment, interruption, contradiction, or unsolicited advice.

☐ D. **Repeat back** (or summarize) what the student is saying so that he or she can reflect upon his or her own thoughts and feelings.

☐ E. **Acknowledge** the student's feelings and perspectives (even if you cannot share their opinion or agree to their requests).

☐ F. **Write it down**: Writing down what someone says is a sign of respect. It shows that we take his/her words seriously, it slows down impulsive thinking, and it provides a visual record to refer back to.

☐ G. **Give genuine praise** ("I'm really proud of you for talking about this").

☐ H. **Introduce a third person** into the process (to bring in a fresh or neutral perspective).

☐ I. **Negotiate and compromise**: Be open to a little give and take.

☐ J. **Set a time frame for the discussion** and, if necessary, make an appointment to continue the discussion at a specific later time and place.

☐ K. **Other:**

7. Rest & Recovery

Refresh & Restart -two valuable options on our computer (and in our lives!)

Think for a moment of a time when you went for too long without sleep. Maybe you were worried about something or maybe you were cramming for a big exam. How did it affect your judgment? Or your reflexes? Your mood? If you are like most people, the longer you went without sleep, the less clear your thinking, and the shorter your fuse. Much like an infant who misses its nap, you might have even become a little "cranky" or "wired."

Now, think of a time when you attended a long lecture on a subject that was very difficult for you (maybe calculus or maybe tax preparation). How did you feel at the end of the lecture? It would not be unusual if you felt completely exhausted, just from trying to absorb all the new information (even though, to an outside observer, you looked like you were just sitting there doing nothing). Maybe you went home and headed straight for your couch, or maybe even straight to bed.

Now think of someone you know who has special needs. Like us, they might sometimes feel exhausted and overwhelmed just from trying to process all the incoming information that bombards them all day, every day. And also like us, they might need to be able to periodically rest, relax, or even sleep.

Sleep is nature's remedy for weariness. It restores our strength, replenishes our spirit, and reboots our nervous systems. We have probably all had the experience of crawling into bed at the end of a long day, worn out and discouraged, but then rising the next morning refreshed and ready to tackle whatever comes our way. And much the same can be said of sleep's younger sibling, the nap. It is truly amazing the effect that a 20-minute power nap can have on the human disposition, almost like pressing the restart button on our internal computer.

Everyone is aware of the benefits that a mid-day rest period has for young children, but we sometimes forget that it can also have a profound impact on older students, on students who might be developmentally younger than their age, and even on ourselves.

7. Rest & Recovery: Provide opportunities for the student to rest, relax, or sleep (preventively or in times of stress).

☐ A. Schedule a **predictable rest time** to occur at, or just before, the time when the student is most likely to need it (for example, midday or upon returning from work).

☐ B. Provide a **safe and respectful place** for the student to rest and regroup (A comfy chair, a recliner, a mat, a couch, the nurses' office, etc.).

☐ C. Provide **enough time** and a **clear time frame** for resting (neither too long nor too short).

☐ D. Provide any **special items** that have been observed to help the person to rest (a blanket, a pillow, a stuffed animal toy, etc.).

☐ E. Provide an environment **suitable to rest** (silence, quiet music, nature sounds, dim lights, natural light, etc.).

☐ F. **Other:**

8. Instruction & Practice (Specific Calming Techniques)

Give a man a fish and he will eat for a day, teach a man to fish, and he will eat for a lifetime. – Maimonides

Just as each of us is unique in the ways that we experience stress, so too are we unique in how we deal with it. For most of human history, people have been trying to find better and better ways to calm and relax. Yoga, for example, was practiced 10,000 years ago. And Meditation dates back at least 1500 BC. Yet both are being rediscovered every day by people to whom they are exciting and new.

Some strategies, such as "taking a deep breath", seem almost too simple to be effective (and yet they work). Others, like "thinking about a happy time or place", are so common that we might not even think of them as being "strategies". Calming strategies do not have to be sophisticated or complicated to be successful. In fact, for most of us, the simpler the better.

The nice thing about teaching calming skills in an instructional situation (before they are actually needed) is that it gives us a chance to try out various strategies in a low-stress (and even fun) environment, and to practice them to the point where they become routine and almost automatic.

Our goal for this strategy is not to see how many different techniques we can teach or learn, but rather to find the one (or ones) that works for an individual student.

8. Instruction & Practice (Specific Calming Techniques): Teach, model, and practice simple strategies for calming, coping, and reducing stress.

☐ A. **Deep breaths:** Teach and model how to take one or more slow, deep, cleansing breaths.

☐ B. Think about a **happy time or place** (visualization): Help the student to picture a happy or relaxing time, place, memory, outdoor scene, movie scene, etc.

☐ C. **Muscle relaxation**: Teach the student to relax his or her body, one part at a time, from the top of their heads to the tip of their toes (my head is relaxed, my neck is relaxed, my shoulders are relaxed, my back is relaxed, etc.).

☐ D. **Count to ten (or any number)**: Counting can sometimes enhance a calming technique by bringing structure and closure to the experience (e. g. "Let's relax to the count of ten", "Let's take three deep breaths", "Let's squeeze our hands five times", etc.).

☐ E. **Yoga**: Yoga is a type of exercise designed to promote health and relaxation. There are many kinds of yoga, including some specifically adapted for children or for students with special needs. Yoga should be taught by a qualified instructor.

☐ F. **Meditation and Mindfulness**: Meditation and Mindfulness are techniques for calming and quieting the body and mind. There are many different types of meditation and many different ways of being mindful, including some specifically adapted for children or students with special needs. Both should be taught by a qualified instructor.

☐ G. **Videos, Apps, and Websites**: Explore videos, apps, and websites that teach and model various calming techniques and/or that present calming sights, sounds, and music (a gentle rain, a flowing stream, a beautiful forest, etc.). Be sure to carefully preview any media that will be viewed by a student.

☐ H. **Other**:

9. Plan B

The best-laid plans of mice and men often go awry. - Robert Burns

It has happened to us all. The dinner that we were planning to serve to our guests gets burnt in the oven. Our vacation plans fall through. We don't get into the college of our dreams. The dog really does eat our homework.

No matter how well we plan an activity or event, something can still always go wrong. As Murphy said in his famous law, "Anything that can go wrong, will go wrong". And when that happens, we all need a "Plan B" (Dinner is burnt? Plan B: Order pizza!).

Just knowing that we have a Plan B increases our confidence and lessens our stress. It is helpful for everyone, but it can be especially helpful for students with special needs, who might not have the cognitive flexibility to handle unexpected changes and disappointments.

Let's take Jenny, for example, a student who was going on a field trip with her class to a local bookstore, expecting to buy her favorite teen magazine. But what if that magazine is sold out? Or what if Jenny's class was planning to stop at the Snack Bar after shopping, but they run out of time? Or what if, just before leaving for the field trip, Jenny starts showing signals of anxiety, difficulty, or distress, and her teacher realizes that it might not be safe for her to go into the community at all?

If Jenny has a Plan B (one that she helped create, and which she regularly reviews with her teacher), she will feel calmer and more in control of any unexpected changes that come her way. And if her teacher also has a Plan B, he or she can feel that same calm confidence.

All of the strategies described throughout this entire process are potential Plan B options. The checklist for this section uses a simple who, what, when, where, and why format to help the team to think through their own Plan B for any given situation. As with most of the strategies that we have discussed, success is often "all in the details".

9. Plan B: Create an alternate schedule or menu of activities that can be used if the student is not ready, willing, or able to participate in the planned activities of his or her day.

Activity	Plan A The original plan:	Plan B The alternative plan:
1. **Who** will I be with?		
2. **What** will I be doing?		
3. **When** will we get started? How long will we be there? When will we be done?		
4. **Where** are we going?		
5. **Why** are we doing this activity? What is our purpose?		

Section IV

Values Check

Section IV

Values Check

It's not hard to make decisions when you know what your values are. - Roy Disney

We are, all of us, kind and caring people who try to treat each other with courtesy and respect, and who strive to do what is best for our students, clients, or family members. And yet, sometimes, even with the best of intentions, it is easy to get so close to a particular situation, or so invested in a particular strategy or outcome, that we "miss the forest for the trees."

When that happens, we sometimes just need to step back and take a look at our decisions through a different lens.

That is what a Values Check is all about. It gives us a chance to reflect upon our own decisions in light of our personal values, current best practices, and community standards.

As with the rest of this process, the questions within the Values Check are designed to be simple, non-technical, and user-friendly. They are designed to spark thoughtful discussion, not to question the team's decisions.

These eight simple questions can be used to reflect upon almost any strategy, plan, or approach that a team is currently using (or considering using), and to ensure that every strategy that we use with our students is safe, sound, respectful and successful.

IV. Values Check

A decision-making tool for ensuring respectful and successful program plans.

1. Is it **safe**? Does this plan protect the student and others from harm?

2. Is it **sound**? Is this plan based upon best practice, research, community standards, and common sense?

3. Is it **respectful**? Does this plan respect the student's age, developmental level, cultural heritage, and personal dignity?

4. Is it **successful**? Does this plan do what it is intended to do?

5. Would you feel comfortable using this plan in a **public place**?

6. Would you feel comfortable using this plan with your own **son, daughter, niece, or nephew,** given the same set of circumstances?

7. Would you use this plan even if you had more **time, money, resources, space, or staffing**?

8. Is it **approved**? Is this plan approved by the student's Individual Educational Planning Team and does it have the informed consent of the student's parent or guardian?

Section V

Writing the Social Learning Profile

V. Writing the Social Learning Profile

One day I will find the right words, and they will be simple - Jack Kerouac

Once our discussion is complete, the next step is to capture the insights, observations, and experiences of the team in a way that can be shared with others, and which can be passed along from year to year, and team to team.

The language used in our worksheets and checklists is designed to provide a structure and a framework for the finished report. The person writing that report should feel free to use the exact phrasing that we have provided for them, but then *personalize* it to the specific student, based on the information gathered from the team's discussion.

Once finished, we suggest running the rough draft back through the team for editing, so that they can help refine the final product. And of course, every plan that addresses a student's behavior should be approved by his or her Individual Educational Planning team and receive the informed consent of his or her parent or guardian.

Note: One additional option to consider, and one that many teams have chosen, is to actually *start* the written report with the student's *strengths and interests*, rather than with his or her specific behaviors of concern (or stress signals).

We all have situations (a job interview, a first date, etc.) in which we try to "put our best foot forward" and to downplay our faults and failings - at least until people get a chance to know us a little better. It's not that we want to *hide* our shortcomings. It's just that we don't want to *lead* with them. Why not give our students that same chance?

By starting the report on a positive note, we are able to present a more complete portrait of the student as someone with strengths, interests, needs, and difficulties (as are we all!); and to put his or her behavior into its proper perspective as being just one small part of who he or she is.

As with everything else in this process, the choice belongs to the team. The following is a possible format for that report.

Name

Social Learning Profile

Date

The following Social Learning Profile is compiled from the collective observations, insights, and experiences of the student's educational team.

I. Areas of Strength & Interest

II. Areas of Need or Difficulty

    1. Specific Behaviors, Problems, or Concerns:

    2. Stress Signals & Distress Signals:

    3. Situations Most Likely:

    4. Situations Least Likely:

    5. Message & Purpose:

    6. Medical & Physical:

    7. Sensory Needs & Issues:

    8. Past Strategies:

III. Success Strategies

    1. Strengths & Interests:

    2. Adaptations & Supports

    3. Space & Environment:

    4. Time & Schedule:

    5. Clear & Visual Information:

    6. Choices & Options

    7. Communication & Self Advocacy:

    8. Attention, Recognition & Respect:

    9. Limits, Rules, & Boundaries

    10. Reward & Incentive:

IV. Calming & Coping Strategies

    1. Calming Tasks & Activities:

    2. Time & Space:

    3. Exercise & Movement:

    4. Respectful Refusals & Dignified Escapes:

    5. Listening & Acknowledgement:

    6. Distraction & Change:

    7. Rest & Recovery:

    8. Instruction & Practice (Specific Calming Techniques):

    9. Plan B:

Section VI

A Simple Data Keeping System

VI. A Simple Data Keeping System

There are many excellent data-keeping systems on the market today, and most school districts and other such organizations, have their own systems integrated into the framework of their planning process. So, we will not attempt to reinvent that particular wheel.

However, we would like to share one simple data-keeping tool that was inspired, many years ago, when we accompanied one of our students (let's call him Joey) to his appointment with his doctor (let's call him Dr. G).

We came to the appointment prepared with reams of graphs, charts, and data concerning Joey's "behavior", which Dr. G glanced through, but then politely handed back to us. He said, "Here's what I want you to do: Take out a piece of paper and write down the numbers 1, 2, and 3. Now, under number 1, I want you to describe Joey *at his best*. Under number 2, I want you to describe Joey when he is *having problems*, but nothing you can't handle. And under number 3, I want you to describe Joey *at his worst*, when he's unsafe, or when none of your best strategies seem to help."

The simple data collection system that we developed from that brief conversation, and which is included here, is one that we still use to this day, many decades later. The next time we met Dr. G, we handed him one simple piece of paper, which could just as easily have been an index card. It said that, in the past month, Joey was at level 1 (at his best) 60% of the time. He was at level 2 (having difficulties, but nothing we could not handle) 32% of the time, and he was at level 3 (unsafe and nothing seemed to help) 8% of the time.

"Excellent!" said Dr. G., "Now my job is to turn those level threes into level twos, so that you can use your strategies to turn those level twos into level ones!"

The data sheets that we provide here have four levels (to correlate with our section on Stress Signals & Distress Signals), but the team may use as many or as few levels as they need. The same sheets may be used to record and summarize specific behaviors of concern, rather than stress levels.

Daily Data Sheet

Name: Date:

1. _____

2. _____

3. _____

4. _____

Time	Rating	Relevant Environmental Information
From: To:		
From: To:		
From: To:		
From: To:		
From: To:		
From: To:		
From: To:		
From: To:		
From: To:		
From: To:		

Weekly Data Sheet

Name: Week of:

1. _____

2. _____

3. _____

4. _____

Time	M	T	W	H	F
from: to:					
from: to:					
from: to:					
from: to:					
from: to:					
from: to:					
from: to:					
from: to:					
from: to:					
from: to:					
from: to:					

Monthly Percentage Summary

Name: Date:

Level	Jan	Feb	March
Level 1			
Level 2			
Level 3			
Level 4			

Level	April	May	June
Level 1			
Level 2			
Level 3			
Level 4			

Level	July	August	Sept
Level 1			
Level 2			
Level 3			
Level 4			

Level	Oct	Nov	Dec
Level 1			
Level 2			
Level 3			
Level 4			

How to Use the Simple Data Keeping Sheets

1. Choose between using the **daily or weekly** data-keeping sheet. The daily sheet has the advantage of providing more room for comments. The weekly sheet has the advantage of allowing the team to view the week as a whole.

2. Choose between recording the student's **stress levels** or **specific behaviors**. Enter those descriptions in the numbered area at the top of the data sheet.

3. Enter the **time frames** to be recorded in the left-hand column of the data sheet (for example by half-hour intervals or by class periods).

4. **If recording the student's stress levels**, enter the number of the *highest level* of stress that the student reached during the given time interval. *Only enter one number.* For example, if Joey were at a level one (calm) for nearly the entire interval, but then briefly reached level three when someone bumped into him in the hallway, enter just the "3" into the box.

5. **If recording specific behaviors**, enter the numbers corresponding to the specific behaviors that occurred during the given time interval (*as many as apply*). For example, if #1 equates to "running" and #2 equates to "hitting", you can enter both 1 and 2 into the box if both occurred.

6. **At the end of the month,** add up the total number of intervals that contain any kind of rating (do not count intervals that are left blank). Then, add up all the intervals that contain a #1 rating, all the intervals that contain a #2 rating, and so on. And finally, calculate each level as a percentage of the total number of entries (e.g., If there were 40 total intervals, and there were 4 intervals containing a level-one rating, then Joey was rated as being at level one 10% of the time.

If you are not math savvy, no worries. Just search for "percentage calculator" on your web browser, and look for one that says something like "_____ is what percentage of _____" (e.g. "4 is what percentage of 40). It is simple, easy, and free. Some examples of completed forms follow:

(EXAMPLE) Daily Data Sheet

Name: Joey   Week of 6/22

1. Calm, friendly, engaged, responsive to direction

2. Fidgeting, pacing, using a loud voice, but still able to follow his schedule

3. Yelling or swearing, unable to follow his schedule.

4. Hitting others, throwing materials

From/To	Rating	Relevant Environmental Information
From: arrival To: 9:00	2	Arrival: Joey arrived from the bus already stressed
From: 9:00 To: 9:30	1	Meeting: Joey seemed to calm down once he settled into the predictable structure of his morning meeting.
From: 9:30 To: 10:00	4	Reading: Joey became distressed as soon as the teacher asked the class to open their book.
From: 10:00 To: 10:30	1	Yoga: Joey calmed quickly, almost as soon as he entered the gym (where Yoga is held).
From: 10:30 To: 11:00	3	Social: Joey's stress escalated almost as soon as the class began.
From: 11:00 To: 11:30	1	Lunch: Hot dogs, french fries, and beans!
From: 11:30 To: 12:00	3	Art: The art activity involved a lot of verbal instructions, directions, and corrections.
From: 12:00 To: 12:30	3	Art: Joey was too frustrated to remain in Art class, he returned to his classroom, and was finally able to relax.
From: 12:30 To: 1:00	1	Work: Joey loves his job, delivering file folders and collecting recycled paper within the school.
From: 1:00 To: 1:30	1	Work: After collecting recycled papers, Joey got to shred them in the paper shredder, another favorite!
From: 1:30 To: departure	1	Rest: After work, Joey returned to class and relaxed until the end of his school day. He left in a happy mood.

(EXAMPLE) Weekly Data Sheet

Name: Joey   Week of 6/22

1. Calm, friendly, engaged, responsive to direction
2. Fidgeting, pacing, using a loud voice, but still able to follow his schedule
3. Yelling or swearing, unable to follow his schedule.
4. Hitting others, throwing materials

Time from/to	M	T	W	H	F
from: arrival to: 9:00	Arrival 2	Arrival 2	Arrival 2	Arrival 3	Arrival 3
from: 9:00 to: 9:30	Meeting 1	Meeting 1	Meeting 1	Meeting 1	Meeting 2
from: 9:30 to: 10:00	Reading 4	Reading 3	Reading 3	Reading 3	Reading 4
from: 10:00 to: 10:30	Yoga 1	Yoga 1	Yoga 1	Yoga 1	Yoga 2
from: 10:30 to: 11:00	Social 3	Social 3	Social 2	Social 2	Social 2
from: 11:00 to: 11:30	Lunch 1	Lunch 1	Lunch 1	Lunch 1	Lunch 1
from: 11:30 to: 12:00	Art 3	Art 3	Art 4	Art 3	Art 4
from: 12:00 to: 12:30	Art 3	Art 2	Art 4	Art 2	Art 2
from: 12:30 to: 1:00	Work 1	Work 1	Work 1	Work 1	Work 1
from: 1:00 to: 1:30	Work 1	Work 1	Work 1	Work 1	Work 2
from: 1:30 to: departure	Relax 1	Relax 2	Relax 2	Relax 2	Relax 1

(EXAMPLE) Monthly Percentage Summary

Name: Joey   Date:

Level	Jan	Feb	March
Level 1	60%	65%	75%
Level 2	20%	15%	10%
Level 3	10%	17%	10%
Level 4	10%	3%	5%

Level	April	May	June
Level 1			
Level 2			
Level 3			
Level 4			

Level	July	August	Sept
Level 1			
Level 2			
Level 3			
Level 4			

Level	Oct	Nov	Dec
Level 1			
Level 2			
Level 3			
Level 4			

References

We are indebted to the work of the pioneers of positive behavioral practices; authors and researchers whose philosophy and writings impacted us early and powerfully in our careers, and who demonstrated that *respect* and *communication* are the most important behavioral tools of all.

Ayres, A. Jean, Ph.D., 1972, "Sensory Integration and Learning Disorders". Western Psychological Services.

Carr, Edward G. and Duran V. Mark, 1985, "Reducing Behavior Problems through Functional Communication", Journal of Applied Behavior Analysis, Vol. 18, pp 111-126.

Donnellan, Anne M. 1984, "Analyzing the Communicative function of Aberrant Behavior", Journal of the Association for Persons with Severe Handicaps, Volume 10, pp 123-131.

Lavigna, G.W. and Donnellan, A.M., 1987, "Alternatives to Punishment: Solving Behavior Problems with Non-aversive Strategies", Irvington Press, New York, New York.

Meyer, Luanna H., and Evans, Ian, 1986, "Modification of Excess Behavior, Education of Learners with Severe Handicaps", Paul H. Brookes Publishing Co.

McGee, John J. 1987, "Gentle Teaching", and "Alternative to Punishment for People with Challenging Behaviors, Teachers College Press.

About the Authors

Jeff Jacobs, M. Ed. is a Special Education Instructor and Behavior Support Teacher who worked for 42 years within Intermediate School District 287 in Minnesota.

Greg Cardelli , MA. Ed, is a Special Education Instructor and Behavior Support Teacher who worked for 37 years within Intermediate School District 287 in Minnesota.

Doug Boeckmann, BA. Psychology, is a Manager with Axis Minnesota Inc., an organization that provides homes and services to individuals with intellectual disabilities. Doug has also worked as a part-time behavioral consultant with Intermediate School District 287 and for various residential homes and schools for 42 years.

— Related AAPC Publishing Books —

To READ the book details and ORDER the book, open the camera app from the Home Screen, hold your device so that the QR code appears in the viewfinder in the Camera app. Tap the notification to open the link associated with the QR code.

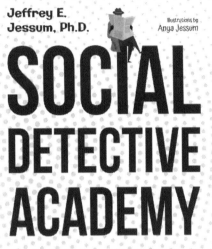

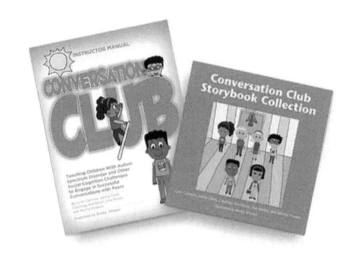

 ISBN: 9781956110104
276 pages

 ISBN: 9781942197355
182 pages

 ISBN: 9781934575840
131 pages

 ISBN: 9781942197027
66 pages

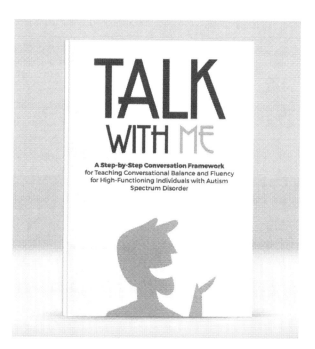

ISBN: 9781942197324

206 pages

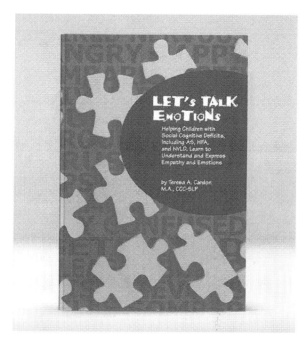

ISBN: 9781931282598

128 pages

ISBN: 9781931282673

368 pages

ISBN: 9781931282819

102 pages

 ISBN: 9781934575314

110 pages

 ISBN: 9781934575864

196 pages

 ISBN: 9781931282918

62 pages

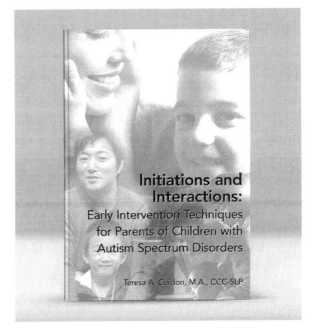

 ISBN: 9781931282321

82 pages

Made in the USA
Columbia, SC
19 July 2022

63727255R00057